The *B*ird, the *F*rog, and the *L*ight

A Richard Jackson Book

The Bird, the Frog, and the Light

a fable by AVI

paintings by

MATTHEW HENRY

Orchard Books   New York

Orchard Books, 95 Madison Avenue, New York, NY 10016

Manufactured in the United States of America. Printed by Barton Press, Inc.
Bound by Horowitz/Rae. Book design by Mina Greenstein.

The text of this book is set in 16 point Weiss Bold. The paintings are rendered in airbrushed acrylic and colored
pencil on Bristol board.

10   9   8   7   6   5   4   3   2   1

Library of Congress Cataloging-in-Publication Data
Avi, date. The Bird, the Frog, and the Light : a fable / by Avi ; paintings by Matthew Henry.   p.   cm.
"A Richard Jackson book"—Half t.p. Summary: A frog learns the truth about his self-importance when he meets
a bird whose simple song brings the sun's light to the world.
ISBN 0–531–06808–0.   ISBN 0–531–08658–5 (lib. bdg.)
[1. Fables.]   I. Henry, Matthew, ill.   II. Title.   PZ8.2.A88Bi   1994   [E]—dc20   93–4886

For *Coppélia*

—AVI

There once was a Bird who greeted the Sun each morning with a song. The Bird's song was nothing very special. It wasn't long or even original. But when the Sun heard it, it beamed with rays of bright light. So it was that each day began.

One morning after the Bird had welcomed the Sun with her song, she heard a voice: "You there, Bird!"

On the ground was a Frog, a great green creature with yellow toes and bulging eyes, each of which looked in a different direction. Upon his head was what appeared to be a golden crown.

"Who are you?" the Bird asked.

"The world's most important king," the Frog replied, puffing up till his belly became huge and his eyes rolled. "You've been lucky enough to have *me* hear you sing to the Sun. I take it you're friends, since it shines on you."

"It likes my song," the Bird replied.

"It's a *ridiculous* song," the Frog King croaked. I'll show you something important."

"Me?"

"Are you deaf, Bird? Don't you realize it's an honor for me to even look at you? Now, follow me!" he commanded.

With that the Frog King heaved himself down a dark hole. The Bird hesitated but decided that if indeed this Frog was important, it would be best to follow.

Down the hole she went. It was so dark she hardly knew which way to step.

"I'll allow you to touch your wing to me," the Frog said. "As usual, I'll lead."

The Bird followed deep below. "Here," said the Frog at last, "is my kingdom. Magnificent, isn't it?"

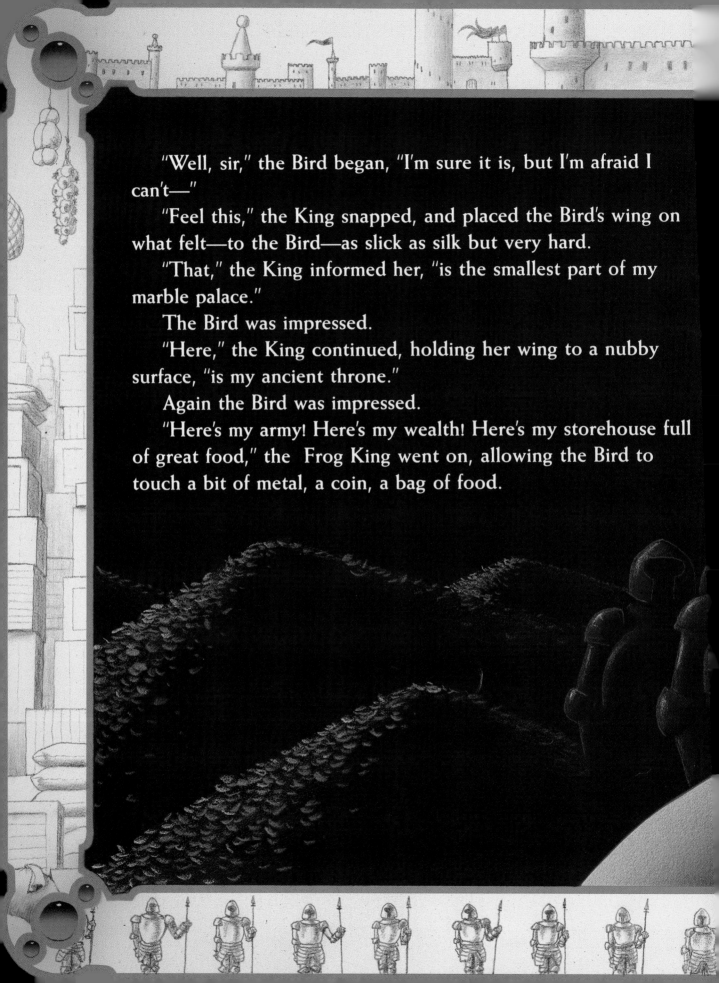

"Well, sir," the Bird began, "I'm sure it is, but I'm afraid I can't—"

"Feel this," the King snapped, and placed the Bird's wing on what felt—to the Bird—as slick as silk but very hard.

"That," the King informed her, "is the smallest part of my marble palace."

The Bird was impressed.

"Here," the King continued, holding her wing to a nubby surface, "is my ancient throne."

Again the Bird was impressed.

"Here's my army! Here's my wealth! Here's my storehouse full of great food," the Frog King went on, allowing the Bird to touch a bit of metal, a coin, a bag of food.

"And here's my library. It's the world's greatest collection of frog wisdom. I'll allow you to touch one page."

The Bird touched it.

"And here in front of you are a million of my loyal subjects."

But before the Bird could meet these loyal subjects, she managed to say, "Please, sir, I felt those things, but I didn't *see* them."

"Exactly!" the Frog King bellowed. "That will be your job."

"I don't understand," said the Bird.

"I'm tired of *feeling* my magnificence," the Frog explained. "I must see it all. I've croaked to the Sun, but my voice is too fine. The Sun won't send me light. Your songs may be ridiculous, but the Sun likes them. You're to fetch one of the Sun's rays and bring it here."

"But sir—"

"Do it or you'll never see the sky again!"

Fearful, the Bird agreed, after which the King guided her back to the earth's surface. "Remember," he warned, "do as you promised, or else."

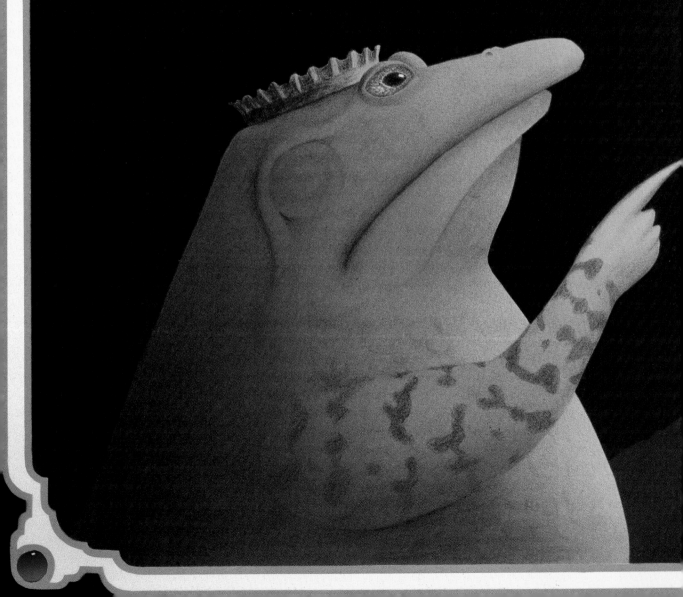

After gathering some leaves, the Bird flew into the sky until she reached the Sun.

"There you are!" the Sun cried. "I've missed your song."

"Was I gone so long?"

"A week!"

"I can't stop to explain," the Bird said. "But please, may I have one of your light rays? I need it for the world's most important king."

The Sun frowned. "That's not a thing I like to do, but"— here the Sun smiled— "you've given me so many songs that I'll make an exception. Take one ray. But be careful. They're hot!"

The Bird plucked a small ray, wrapped it carefully in the leaves, then flew back to the earth.

The Frog King was waiting impatiently. "What took you so long?" he croaked, so excited he puffed himself up three times his normal size. Down the hole he bolted, tight squeeze though it was. The Bird followed.

Once below, the King cried, "Now, throw the ray up so I can see my greatness!"

The Bird unwrapped the ray and deftly flung it up. The higher it sailed, the brighter it grew, casting light in all directions.

The Bird looked about. Instead of a marble palace, all she saw was a small rock, smooth from constant rubbing. The throne was a chicken roosting box. The army, nothing but a tin can. And fabulous food? A small bag of beans. Treasure? One penny. A million loyal subjects? No one was there but the Frog King and the Bird. As for the library, it proved to be just one page from the telephone book.

"Stop!" cried the Frog King. "Put out the light! Put out the light!"

"I can't," the Bird said. "It's burning too fiercely."

In desperation, the Frog King snatched off his crown and heaved it at the ray of light. When the crown struck it, it shattered the light, sending down brilliant multicolored sparks.

Once again there was complete and utter darkness. Then the Bird heard the King. He was sobbing. "Can't even read," he admitted in a whisper.

The Bird made her way back to the top of the earth. When she reached it, she was just in time to greet the rising Sun with her song. She was about to begin when she heard a sound. It was the Frog King.

"Please," the Frog croaked, "would you . . . could you teach me . . . to read?" And he held up the torn page from the telephone book.

The Bird flew down and picked up the page. It was from the letter R. "R," the Bird began.

"R is for . . . ridiculous!" snapped the Frog, and he began to swell again.

"R is for reading," the Bird insisted.

The Frog sighed, letting out most of his air. Then he croaked, "R is for reading."